The Moments, the Minutes, the Hours

The Moments, the Minutes, the Hours

THE POETRY OF
JILL SCOTT

Jill Scott

St. Martin's Griffin
New York

www.stmartins.com

Book Design by Susan Walsh

Library of Congress Cataloguing-in-Publication Data

Scott, Jill, 1972–
    The moments, the minutes, the hours : the poetry of Jill Scott.
        p.cm.
    ISBN-13: 978-0-312-32962-4
    ISBN-10: 0-312-32962-8
        I. Title

PS3619.C666 M66 2005
811'.6—dc22

                                              2004058532

First St. Martin's Griffin Edition: April 2008

10 9 8 7 6 5 4 3 2 1

Some say that life is a gift

A time to learn and rethink what was a thought in our before minds

Some say that life is a simple series of minutes moments hours days

weeks

years seconds

time

A space to live and then to die

I say Yes

Yes Lord

Yes to all the heady stuff in between.

  —JILL SCOTT

Table of Contents

List of Illustrations

Will Downing's photographs appear on pp. 112, 119, 124
Web site: www.WILLDOWNING.com
Violinist on Street (p.119) "featuring Verve Recording Artist,
   Regina Carter."
Profile of little girl (p. 124) "SIOBHAN"

Eric McLaurin (SAGAMOOR)—photographs appear on pp. 25, 33,
   34, 37, 41, 89
Contact info: the_sagacontinues@yahoo.com
(267) 334-2743

Riva's photograph of Jill Scott on p. 113

Joshua Mays's paintings appear on pp. 9, 68, 91, 97, 116
Web site: www.soldren.com
e-mail: joshua@soldren.com

Stacey Wilson's paintings appear on pp. 44, 61, 73, 79, 95
e-mail: squarebiz.org and flyjawn.com

American flag photograph on p. 101 is provided by Siede Preis/Getty
   Images.

Introduction

GLORY TO GOD AND ALL BLESSINGS TO HIM.

Thank you for buying this book. It is truly a pleasure to see this longtime dream come to light. For several years I have wanted to create a book of my poetry. I began writing poetry after my eighth grade teacher Ms. Fran Danish gave an extra credit assignment. She gave us each a sheet of paper with a list of forty names and asked that we write an essay about one person. I didn't need the extra credit (at the time) but I thought it couldn't hurt because I wanted to go to a "good" high school. The list was long so I closed my eyes and swung my finger around and landed dead smack on Nikki Giovanni. I thought it was some Italian lady and considered swinging my finger around again but I had done enee menee minee mo to make my choice and that, in the eighth grade, was sacred. So later that day I went to my school library and found absolutely nothing. I was intrigued because Albert M. Greenfield library, at my new fancy school, usually had all the information I needed, but Ms. Danish (the best teacher on the planet) did say that this assignment would be different. So, I walked to 25th St. and LeHigh and visited my neighborhood library. I usually didn't like the library in the hood because it didn't have the bright colors or the comfy chairs like the ones at my school but I went anyway. The nice lady behind the counter knew exactly who I was talking about and quickly handed me a small book. I opened it and was instantly excited to find that this Nikki Giovanni person was a Sista. On the first page there was a picture of a young girl getting her hair brushed by a grandmother figure. There was also a poem called "Legacies." I completely recognized the story inside the poem. Although I had never seen this book or heard of this woman, but I knew the experience like my mother's perfume. There were other poems like "Winter Poem" in which Ms. Giovanni describes being one with nature. I loved to cry in the rain. I loved to read in the sun. I loved to kiss snowflakes too. By reading these poems I felt I was a part of something big instead of just a ghetto girl in a fancy school.

I felt riveted to read something so close to my own experiences. I mean yeah, we read Emily Dickinson (who is quite fly by the way), and of course Shakespeare but Nikki Giovanni's poetry felt specifically designed for me. I know that sounds narcissistic but I had found my first love and life became all about us. My appetite was ravenous and after the assignment was turned in, I began to do more research on Black Poets. I found out about this guy named Gil Scott-Heron and he wrote a poem (he later made into song), called "Paint It Black." When I read "Paint It Black" I felt the sad honesty inside the words. I felt angry. I felt distressed and, for that moment, I somewhat understood what it must be like to be a poor Black Man in America. The poem allowed me to see how desperate living in poverty can be and the strength a man must have to maintain his sweet soul in a country that doesn't respect him. "Paint It Black" is a short poem but definitely troubling and deeply profound.

Around the same age, I also discovered Langston Hughes who wrote poems like "Aunt Sue's Stories" and "Red Silk Stockings." When I read "Aunt Sue's Stories" I thought of the women in my own family, Shirley and Mom-Mom, Annie and my own mother. So many stories to share; so much laughter, so many tears. I still smile when I read "Aunt Sue's Stories" but when I read "Red Silk Stockings," I actually feel sick to my stomach. It recalls memories of liking a certain dark-skinned boy and hearing my own family members say, "Oh no Jill, he too black and Lord Lord what would them babies look like?" This poem brings back painful memories of hot combs burning my ears and the threat of clothespins on my nose. At fourteen I felt awakened. So with all these thoughts, roaming around my mind, I, too, began to write.

I adored writing my own poetry. I bought the ninety-nine cent composition books (which I still use) and filled book after book with ideas and strange feelings that were happening in my young body. I watched my community for inspiration, my mother's face, people on the bus, "the change" when crack and "crack heads" became the norm. I felt like I was in this private miraculous world of words but as special as I thought my writing was, I wasn't quite ready to share it with other people. I just believe in taking my own time. However, one summer my cousins snuck in my room and read my special words to the boys in the neighborhood and I was so humiliated I vowed not to write again. So I stopped. Years went by and I didn't even open the books that I had created (but I was singing honey, so no poor me). Then as a young adult, unfortunately and quite fortunately, I had my heart ripped to shreds. I say "unfortunately" because it hurt like a mother. It was such a horrible slap to my young ego, I almost lost me but I say "fortunately," because I began to write again. I wrote to get the stench of love lost off of my being. I wrote because crying was not sufficient. I wrote basically to save the me I had grown to appreciate. And once again, I found words utterly freeing.

At college I became a secondary English major. My plan was to teach English Literature to high school students and offer the same prize Ms. Danish had offered me but it wasn't working out the way I planned. Paying tuition was not at all easy. Yeah there were grants and scholarships and I had two jobs but the effort of paying for school seemed to outweigh the benefits of actually going. So I quit and got a job with the hopes of moving out of my mom's basement. I went to work. I sold clothes at French Connection. I became an assistant manager and it was cool. I had fly clothes and some money so I liked my job but I was looking for "something." A few months after my promotion, we hired a young woman named Gail and Gail introduced me to another poet. Her name was Tiffany Clark. We hit it off right away. We became "Clark and Scott."

Together we were brave and read our poetry everywhere we could;

parties, picnics, coffee houses, libraries, and of course art galleries. We made very little money but mostly we got our weight (performance skills) up and had a great time. Eventually it was time for us to go our separate ways. She went off to California and I stayed in Philly. There were a few places to read that absolutely seemed otherworldly. The focus was real. Blue Funk, The Bridge hosted by the incredible J. Michael Harrison, Butta Milk at the North Star Bar and The October Gallery were the places where the poets met. We all wanted to be better poets. Stephanie Renée, Trapeta Mayson, Rich Medina, Ursula Rucker, Lamar Manson (Black Ice), and Sabela were just a few of the poets who, to me, were already electric. We were all so different in our writing styles and subject matter but we were connected in a truly powerful powerful way. We were Poets. Igniting minds, shaping pictures, calling out, sometimes begging, praising, and admonishing. We were Poets and we still are. It is my pleasure to dedicate this book to Ms. Fran Danish, my eighth-grade teacher, and all the poets of Philadelphia, New York, and Washington D.C. who continue to insight, ignite, and recite this blessed, raunchy, wild ride of a craft. Poetry.

To all other poets on the planet—write like there's no tomorrow. If you do not, there may not be.

I

"All the Evil and All the Love"
—MISTER ON SHUG AVERY, *The Color Purple*

Across Your Bread

I'm juss gon say what I need to
juss gon put it on the table
And spread it across your bread

As much as I didn't want
I have stumbled
tripped
fallen ova myself in love with every molecule of
you

The walk on you
The way you out then in breathe
Simply your eyes man
got my thighs swellin' and my knees beggin' to part
I do (shaking my head up and down)
I do
love everything about you
All that makes you you
And what I do not know, I swear I will love too
If you just show me

I know it's crazy but I swear
My heart doesn't pump blood
When you are not near me
I juss walk my way through life comatose
Till I hear my name in your key
I juss stay
Hoping, wishing, praying for the moment you say it's cool for me to
give you what I got
Cool for me to give you what I keep
Cool for me to give you what is fresh behind the apples

And the pears but you don't
      Won't
Accept it then accept it then return it
My logic understands but my back is tired of the weight
My feet are swollen and my fingers ache from writing

Don't you see?
I'm willing
      Willing
To go that extra continent
      Willing
To carry that extra gallon and love that extra kind
I am placing myself on the table
Spreading myself across your bread
So, say something
It's your move

The Last Time

You
My first love
My first kiss
My first experience
There have been others since
But still we sex
When I don't have a love
Even when you might

You
My constant
My anytime
My easy fix
Continuous
You know me
Memorized the spell
You used when I was sixteen
Pull it from thin air
Whenever you'd like
What I do

You
Heat and passion
Us
Bodies banging
Waves crashing
We kiss like we used to
We move and grind like we used to
We grip and hold
We inhibition free too
And then I remember
I'm not sixteen anymore

Potty Trained

I pushed and
I grunted and
I labored and
I squeezed and
You splashed and
I cleaned and
I stood and
I flushed
and
I don't even think of you now

The Downfall of a
North Philly Freak

As he walked into the room
I felt her stiffen
I knew this was just the type she liked
Handsome brotha
Brown, tall, regal
Sexy brotha
Smelling good like hot sex on Sunday after church
Soooo wrong but soooo right
I knew she would weaken
I knew she would fall short of the promise she made
After that
Other brotha "loved"
split her apart
And left her drowning in her own self
I knew she didn't mean what she said
I tried to hold her but she slid from the
satin lining

It has been 6 whole days
and
she hasn't checked in
once

Young Buck Lovin' on the Kitchen Floor

He thought cuz he had split it
That he had did it
Thought he took her to heaven's gate
Thought he shined the right shoe
And put it on the good foot
Thought with all his testosterone pumping
His hips popping and jumping
That he had taken her on the ride of the millennium
Plus some
And
although he Had pounced on her body
      "hit that"
      "tapped that"
      "wore that out"
with new passion and speed
all he truly managed to do
was make it sting when she peed

Kings at Clubs?

Every Friday night
My sistas are going to the Funky Blue Jazz Club on 42nd and
Whatever
wearin' dresses too
short
too tight
too small
paradin' fat rounds up and down
like proud peacocks on the stroll
they rolling eyes and sweeeaaarrrin'
that their swing is better than the next girl and the next to her
while waiting in them long lines to add extra to
made-up faces

And there he is—the fantasy
He knows
if they see him looking fly—
they'll think he's fly—and he'll fake fly
until he can peel off her
too short
too tight
too small dress
and place another notch
on his cramped bedroom wall
he just looks so good in his fly shit
that they forget to remember
and wonder after he's plowed that tass a few times
why doesn't he call anymore.

Pocket-Size #1

You wanted some
Thought you could get some
Shoulda earned some
But you tried to take some
That was dumb
Keep breathing jackass
The ambulance will be here soon

The Sound of Your Name

Last night while I slept alone in our bed,
I dreamed of you
Your head was cocked to the side
And you were smiling at someone
But I couldn't see who
I called out your name
I called out to you
I woke to the sound of your name
Falling

He says

He says that I'm beautiful
But it's deeper than brothers
Honkin horns
blowin kisses
Buyin drinks

He says my beauty can be seen even better with his eyes closed
And
Every now and then
he swears he can touch my beauty but he says
He's not worthy and he's glad I can't see that

He says he likes my style
Feminine with a little rugged
Just enough lady mixed with ghetto chic and urban funk

He says I'm powerful with poetry
The way I use ordinary words and make them sing
He hums my songs

He says he knows me
Favorite number—4
Favorite color—black
Favorite juice—peach
Favorite style—free

He says he loves the way I make love
With my whole self
Imploring, no, demanding he do the same

He says that I constantly make myself new and better
he loves that quality
and do I think that maybe one day possibly
I could spend my life with him

He says he loves me
I say I'm just lucky and I'm glad
he can't see that

Radio Blues

Do me

Screw me

Tease me

Please me

Freak me

Leash me

Lick me

Suck me

Oh God, where arc the love songs?

It's the Little Things

While Grandma made her famous fried chicken
The tiny hairs in her nostrils began to tingle and twitch
No holds barred in her own kitchen
She stuck her pointer finger deep
scratching the bothersome itch
She went left then right
Then round and round
Her finger steadily growing wet
"Hmm" her only sound
She plucked into the trash
She washed her hands and when the chicken
The greens, the potatoes were prepared
and done she made Grandpa's plate
She didn't have to do anything in that order
It's the little things

Pocket Size #4

Baby

I don't understand why you try to hide our love

Love is like farting in a crowded elevator

People may not see who's doing it

But they sure can smell it

Pocket Size #5

I didn't dial your number
because I needed someone to talk to
Arms to lay in
Or sweet words to fill my ears
I didn't call you because I can't hook up my speakers
or kill the spider above my bed
I was just wondering why
you haven't called

Old School Lovin'

While you were out
I realized how much . . .
I mean
How good us is
So I want to share
Something my momma taught
A skill for loving—the wild and wicked kind
I think you are deserving
So I practiced and I know it's tight
You used to say
My mom was a freak
And yes you were right
So get comfortable
Close both eyes
Open your mouth
And taste
My scratch sweet potato pie

Caution

It's been nice
Yes
Laughing times
Early morning love
Walks
Meaningful kissing
But I've been hurt before
The kind that can change a life
The kind that makes a body wary
And I must say that I am taking special care
Not to care so hard

While I am mostly open to love you
I prepare to let you go
So I will ask upfront
Before my stomach is knotted

Can I take my shoes off now?
Can I put them next to yours in the upstairs closet?
Can I relax my soles?
Hang up my winter coat?
Unpack my bag for more than the night?
Because
I like you
I really like you

Agape

10

    11

        12

           1, 2, 3 o'clock

no show no call

November

December

January

February

March

Mid-April the phone rings

I still love him

Untitled #1 (Love Sucks)

You constantly break me down,
Cut me open and turn me inside out
Therefore, my feelings are equal to hell
Their foulness haunts me like a backed-up cesspool
Reeking of used tampons
Vomit
Baby diarrhea ditties
Drunken old man's piss
And filth.
Despite the stench
Despite the nausea
I love you still
Please call soon,

Love,
Dummy

Pocket Size #8

My name is Jill Scott
His name is SHHHHHHH
My name is Jill Scott
His name is SHHHHHHH
I went to write my name
And wrote SHH and stopped
I think I'm a fool in love

Dis Niggah (for Leslie)

Dis niggah done broke my heart
Done played my tune double-time
So I sinned and sinned and...sinned again
Got caught up
Gave in

Dis niggah done took my sugah
Left me a half a spoon
Can't make no Kool-Aid from foolin' with dat fool
Wanna get my stuff back but a niggah can't be found
Niggahs don't have no daytime schedule
So you never know when a niggah gon be round

Niggahs talk too loud but don't say shit
Wanna make a niggah a man
But a niggah just don't want it

Blue

I put food coloring in my bath yesterday
Sat in a pretty blue
Let the drops fall from my finger tips
Onto my breast and my stomach
I just wanted to look how I feel
Without you

Selfish

give me a minute to love you
an hour to stare in your face
a moment to praise your nose
your hands, your lips, your eyes
don't say later
don't say tomorrow
because the day's too busy
because the day's too hurried
too demanding

give me a week to hold you
a second to play in your lashes
a night to kiss your forehead
Your back, your feet, your fingers
Don't say you're tired
Don't say you're anxious
because the world is calling
because the world is heavy
Ever present

just let me soothe you
let me put you in my mouth and hum sweet tunes
let me calm that ocean

give me a day
give me four and more
to ease and please you
let me take that chip from your shoulder
place it on the nightstand for a while
because you're lonely
and
I am too

Revolutionary Man

I am grown now
A woman
Got my house
Got my car
Gotta cat too
Yeah!
But I needs me a man
Like air
Like wa ta
Yeah!
(I ain't trying to impress you)
I needs me a breakfast makin',
Long walkin', Black movie watchin',
Conversationalist
Yeah!
I needs me a standing up
Accept no bullshit (cept mine) man
An honest, hair brushing
Public kissin, praying on his knees man
Respect full
Protect full
Full-grown man
Yeah!
Laughin' anda working,
Ain't afraid to feel man
Ain't afraid to be afraid man
Ain't afraid to be strong
Revels in it
Needs me a soldier
Yeah!
Needs me some passion
Needs me a revolution in my bed

Haiku # 6

Just the other day
I thought about you so hard
I blew my ice cream

One Second of Warped Security

I was chillin' with him on a Sunday

It was a good day

All day makin' love day

I didn't think

That I could feel that safe

That comfortable

That secure

But

I did

And

HIV came to visit

Nothing Is for Nothing

i had be turning tricks Long before i actually knew it
Being whatever They wanted me to be
Whenever They wanted me to be it
A Freak
Inside
Outside
kitchen counters
Laundry mats
2 at a time
Hotels
Motels
and backseats of leased cars, vans and jeeps

made myself like it
cuz They liked it and i liked that They liked it
so
        i continued being the perfect image of a wet dream
nasty
wild
exotic
erotic
Freak was what They wanted
so
Freak was who i was

and Everybody walked and talked about me
like technology wasn't raping our children
like welfare and teenage pregnancy wasn't becoming synonymous
with being Black and woman
like there was nothing to talk about but what i was doing or screwing
but i was content giving my men a little heaven between
their struggle to breathe
and contemplation of suicide

wasn't i good for the cause?

Closed mind

Open legs

Making niggaz forget why they so damned angry

Wasn't i good?

Then the mood swung as well the tempo

And i became an ideal

They wanted her

Soft spoken

Sweet and generous

Pretty and docile

Caring and stupid

So there i was

ready for action

on your Mark

Seth

Joe...and i was Suzy homemaker on the hunt for love

cooking and cleaning

washing and ironing

faithful

and a Freak in the bedroom

cuz that's what They liked and i liked being what They liked

so what They liked was who i was

a prostitute

selling my soul for emotional gain

Struggling not to be the third generation

of lonely women in my family

Struggling to gain but gaining nothing but confusion

frustration

pain

illusion

and emptiness

cuz there was no love
just condom wrappers on the floors to be discarded
like me

a prize performer long before i knew it too
cuz i was faking me out of the me i would become
the ME that I see (thank You God!)
now
the ME who holds on to herself with both hands and all feet
the ME who must have love
and give it (thank You God)

the ME who brings more to the table than good looks and a wet hole
the ME that is confident and
intelligent, shit I might as well say it
brilliant and
filled to the brim with love and respect
for
ME

And...

a freak
Cuz that's what I like and
I like being what I like and
what I like
Is all a part of who I am.
Dig ME?
Well I definitely do.

II

HAIKU

Haiku #1

It was a loud cry
When I was brought to this world
Been loud ever since

Haiku #2

Occasionally
I wish I could whip your back
But that won't help me

Pride

Respect

Family

Haiku #3

Hop skip jump dummy
Do that dance they like to see
But it won't be me

Motivation

Dignity

Pride

Knowledge of Self

H a i k u # 4

I hear you Thinking
Thinking things to pull me down
I love anyway

Haiku #5

I hear them say it
Cuss words ain't for no lady
But sometimes shit's real

III

I BE THINKING

Lab Animal (from Inside the Cage to You)

All right
I'm not gon try to get it anymore
Because I do believe I understand you
All this thinking for such a simple science
What does a bee do when the flower blooms?
What does the alley cat do when the unchained dog
begins to growl?
I do believe I understand it now
I would be attracted to me too
I would be afraid of me if I ever got free too
I would create the bars and the locks and the chains and
work so things won't change too if I were you
Just know that I am not
Blind anymore
Busy wasting my time no more
Busy trying to understand you
I'm too busy understanding me
And you will always be afraid and we both know that

Don't we

Searching

Tell me

Make it make sense to my tired mind

Write it down

Spell it out

Correct grammar please

Do this for me because I need to understand how it is

How it is

That the words we live through

Those words written in script erstwhile

Sacred and brilliantly satisfactory

Are now void and defunct

Explain that!

Tell me!

Make it make sense to this tired mind!

Write it down

Spell it out

Correct pronunciation please

Do me a solid

Explain how it is

How it is

That the church where we bow our heads

And sanctify

Is nasty vile

Filled with liars on pulpit

And destroyers of innocence

Explain that

My mind says that we are all but men

Fault full and pitiable

Yet my heart knows we are as great as we deem

However we excommunicate our conscious for this single day

This exorbitant pay

But the day can be more colorful and peaceful
More vivid
More fruitful
I know and can't prove
but by my living
and offering up this soul that You have kindly given to me
and I know I should be patient but still I get so angry
cuz
We are falling deeper
Into Sadness and desperate personalities
Needing salvation in a pill, a bottle
a dick
That just stands up quick
And infects with precision

God bless my mind
Make me understand
Tell me
Make it make sense
Write it down once again
Correct and simple grammar please
Explain to me how it is
How it is

Little Man in a Box
(Catholicism)

LITTLE MAN IN A BOX
DO YOU GET SCARED?
AFRAID OF THE DARK
WHAT LEARS BEHIND SHADOWS
DEEP IN THE HEART PARTS?

DO YOU GET LONELY LITTLE MAN
WAKE UP TO YOUR HANDS
IN HIDDEN PLACES
DO YOU THINK STRANGE THANGS
WANT TO "CHA CHAY YEE YOK"
SAY THINGS FROM SOMEWHERE
YOU AIN'T SEEN
NEVER TOUCHED?

DO YOU PEE IN HOLES?
SWEAT
WASH YOUR SOCKS?
COUNT NICKELS AND DIMES IN YOUR HAND
CLIP YOUR FINGERNAILS
ARRANGE YOUR SCHEDULE
OPEN THE DOOR WITH A KEY
IN A LOCK?

LITTLE MAN IN A BOX
DO YOU FEEL AS LITTLE AS I DO?
HOLD YOUR SHOULDERS FUNNY
WHEN THANGS ON YOUR MIND
DO YOU BLINK WHEN THE SUN SHINE YOUR FACE?
DO YOU TASTE GRAPES AND MARVEL
AT THE SOFT INSIDE

SWEET THIN BUT THICK
WASH THEM
PUT THEM IN A BOWL
EAT THEM UNDER A TREE
OFF THE VINE
WHEN THERE'S TIME LIKE ME?
DO YOU GET THIRSTY?

LITTLE MAN IN A BOX
HIDDING THERE
BEHIND THE SCREEN THING
ARE YOU DRINKING COFFEE ON THE OTHER SIDE
DO YOU FEEL PRIDE? ARE YOU SHY?
HAVE YOU RELIEVED YOUR SHOES FROM YOUR FEET
ARE YOU NEAT?
AND ALL THE WHILE YOU SAY "CONFESS MY CHILD"
BUT I AM ASKING
WHO
ARE YOU HERE . . . ANYWAY?

YOU ARE INSIDE A BUILDING
BEHIND A RED DOOR
THAT NOWADAYS GETS LOCKED
BUT ME...
TEMPTATION LICKS MY EVERYDAY EYES
FRUSTRATION HOWLS AT MY FRONT DOOR
REALITY SO BOLD AND SAUCY
I GET HIGH JUST TO CRY
SO
I'M CONFUSED BY YOU LITTLE MAN IN A BOX
CROSS-EYED AND CROSS SIDE
IS YOUR FAITH STRONGER THAN MINE?
DO YOU KNOW THINGS MY GUT DON'T KNOW?

DO YOU HAVE SOME INVITATION I HAVE FORGOTTEN TO
   RECEIVE?

YOU DON'T KNOW ME
BUT I DO
BELIEVE
GOD IS ALL WHERE
THROUGH
BEYOND
OVER
KNOWS MORE THOROUGHLY
GENUINE MORE SURELY
DON'T HIDE BEHIND NO DOOR
INSIDE A BUILDING
WITH WINDOWS TELLING STORIES
BIG CROSS SYMBOLS, IDOL GLORY
AS PLAIN AS THE EYE CAN SEE
GOD WITH ANY NAME FORGIVES FREELY
WITHOUT
YOU
OR
3 HUNDRED
HAIL
MARYS

Pocket Size #3

Brothas
Just because you've loved and lost don't mean stop lovin'
If you have a nightmare,
Does it mean you stop dreaming?

My Life

My name is Jill. Scott, A white name but I am not. I look like a girl
at 30 years old. Maybe my insides are showing. I think that's good.
I see wonderment in lovemaking and flowers and children and
people and music and pain. This earth, for me, has been a phantasm
of brilliance; so abundant and passionate that I cry when I do not
expect. My God, you are good. I have laughed until cramps in
London and Germany, smoked amazing weed in Toronto and
Amsterdam, read my own poetry in my own way, wrote songs under
trees on benches while watching pigeons copulate and I dug it all.
I am a blessed woman, yes I am. I've met people, seen people and
looked through some. I do not hide well. My feelings show on my
face. I think I should change but that quality has been mine all of my
life. Sometimes I do not communicate well, so many emotions. I get
angry. I get annoyed. Met some brilliant folks: actors, vocalists,
healers, writers, artists, children, so many, that I know God is real.

I am an artist. I cannot help it. I do not read music. Don't know
how. I just wait for the music to move me, adjust my thinking, shape
my voice. I sing my life. I live in music.

Life

I had been running
Running on this path
Knew it to be small and rugged
However, I wanted to go on this path.
So I was running
        running
        running on this path and I saw an opening
And I was glad
Relieved
I believed
Believed there would be joy
For me
There
So I was running
        running
        running on this path
And in the distance
I could see
Light
Excited
I kept running
        running
        running on this path
And when I arrived
There were stairs

Life

Pink Man's Redemption

And Caucus looked from his mountaintop
Pink skinned from the cold, crown self-righteously thin
And decided that he alone was good
In his hands, rocks and sticks
In his blue heart and eye
Hatred for Father God and Mother Nature
For recognizing their only error and banishing him
To his mountain so high
His hatred grew into obsession
His obsession grew into hatred and he was reborn
Unto into himself
All righteous
All wondrous
All glorious

ssssslowly he slithered down
Onto lush peaceful greens, yellows to browns
Disease and greed filled
He disguised himself as the All Mighty
And multiplied times himself
Injecting tainted blood into melanin painted life
Dividing and distributing his damnation
And he was redeemed
All righteous
All wondrous
All glorious

He destroyed what was Godly
And remade the world in his own image
Redefining what was natural
Desecrating what was beautiful
Placing his woman
Pink skinned from the cold

Crown self righteously thin next to the definition
And the world began to stink
A violent heaving stench that spoiled the air
And made all fruit born rotten
And he was redeemed

As his greed spread
He became drunk with the very essence
of first man
Red faced and staggering
He constantly craved the blood of
colored things as entertainment
He murdered for comedy
Amputated for pleasure and raped for lust
In its animal form
He pillaged, plundered and plucked up
all roots from greens to yellows to
browns making once upright souls sag
with burden never meant to carry
And he was redeemed
All righteous
All wondrous
All glorious
And he was redeemed

Untitled

Sometimes I swear
I can hear my past thundering toward me like a herd of elephants
I cover my ears and look the other way but it still wants to come up
Like rotten milk

Untitled #2 (for MTV Black History Month 2001)

Can't do that dance anymore
It doesn't fit my size, never did
I'm too big to do that dance
Always was too pretty
Won't shuck and jive
Not gonna coon
Not I
Too many ancestors' tear stains on my face
Too many claps and hallelujahs under my belt
Not for anybody's enjoyment
Not for anybody's money
Green or long
Pound or euro
Not for you
Not I
I don't have time to do that dance
There aren't libraries in my baby's school
Playgrounds filled with glass
Teachers who are waiting for me to show up
And I will...on time

You won't catch me doing that dance
Not in this honey dwelling
I live here
My mother and God designed this for me
Just enough cinnamon (blow a kiss)
Just enough nutmeg (blow a kiss)
Stirred me in a pot
Listened for the timing bell
Ring and I am ready
Bite me when I'm cool

Bite me again when I'm not
Bite me all you want because
I've got more and some more and some more
And I will not do that dance
Not for you
Not for you
Too much to do that dance
And I am way too pretty

Untitled #3 (in progress)

It appears now that 8th St. won't lead to my destination
No El train or sub to pause at my stop
No hacks outside the market
No maps in the gas station
No locals to point the way
No green for go either
But I must arrive

It looks now that no strong man muscles will carry my luggage
No rough hand will rip the vines from my path
No big prints to follow in the sand
No shoulders to ride on
Or open pockets for fare either
But I must arrive

I Forgive You

I practice
I open my mouth wide for the "I"
Stick my bottom lip in for the "for"
Touch the roof of my mouth with my tongue
For the "give" and get stuck
"I forgive you"
I practice
Looking in the mirror for honest eyes
And a relaxed way when the words come
She didn't mean it I say
She didn't know I say
But you knew
You're so smart
You knew that this trouble would bubble in me
That I would need to pass this gas
You knew my pant size would climb
You knew my limited sleep would tense
And ultimately I would do it
I would forgive you
But I hate you for knowing me so well

Space

And they said "BECAUSE YOU HAVE NO PENIS,
You need a place, a spot, a cage, boundary lines"
With a fall of a gavel
Some who do voodoo
Backward words and a tug on my womb (as a reminder of it) they
Gave me a triangle with a bright gray bow and a sign
"WE DECLARE THIS BODY, THIS FORM SHALL HOLD ONLY
SUCH AND SUCH FROM THIS TO THIS TIME"
But 3 sides could not hold me
Too cramped, too smashed, too mashed inside
Couldn't breathe
Needed space
Room for these thick hips
These heavy lips
And this solid mammary pair
They shook their necks, scratched their asses, threw gray streamers
In the air and gave me a sign
"THIS SIMPLE INTELLECT, THIS SMALL MIND SHALL
HOLD
ONLY SUCH AND SUCH FROM THIS TO THIS TIME"
But the 4 sides could not hold me
Too tight, not right, not enough space inside
Too heavy for the bottom of that box
Too beautiful for their gray chains and locks
I scream but heard a whisper
"Let me out. let me out"
Slam the gavel shout
"YOU ARE NO ONE"
And with the blinking of an eye I was in an octagon
Along with a sign
"IT IS DECREED THAT THIS MAN'S TOOL, THIS FOOL
SHALL
HOLD ONLY SUCH AND SUCH FROM THIS TO THIS TIME"

But 8 sides could not hold me

Too strong, too much love, too much pride

And not even this space had enough space inside

So I pushed and pushed with my full lips, my heavy thighs and my

Solid mammary pair

I rubbed, scraped, Brillo-ed the surface of that cell with my nappy

Hair

I pressured, I pinched, I screeched and I shout till the whole man

World can't stand my noise, my undying persistence and then...

I was out

Free to pick up my brush and paint my soul free

Free to dance my freedom dance free

Free to sing my freedom song free

Free to reach my hands in all directions free

Free to move my legs free

Free and in control free

So I take my freedom walk

Stroll up and down my freedom road

Shaking my freedom ass

Smiling my freedom smile

Praying on my freedom knees

Only to look up and find

Glass

Why Rape

To cut
It
To crush
It
To beat
It
To slice
It
To jab
It
To burn
It
To slash
It
To crack
It
To splice
It
To rip
It
To stab
It
To kill
It

The present soul
The treasured spirit

IV

US SISTAHS SOMETIMES

Envy

You should see her
She got hips that sway and dance for no good earthly reason
Lord make me just like her
No
No make me better
Make me the kind that can change the weather
Stop tornados
And heavy storms from tearing down the shingles
I want to stop traffic
I want them to moan and lust
I want to be bold and sexy sexy like that
Make me "hot" like they say on videos
I want to be a 12 out of 10
No a 14
Shooot make me a 25
Then I know I'll be happy
Just like Halle Berry

Perms, Hot Combs, and Curlers

"get it out" I say
"5 more minutes" she say
"get it out" I say
"5 more minutes if you want it straight"
blisters, sores, peels
I pick
Leaving lighter designs underneath
I burn because I want my pride to blow in the summer wind
I burn because I want silky, fancy-free shining glorious assimilation
And maybe too cuz it seems easy
I lay toxin thick
Over and over ends split
I drive down
Beat less my own attractiveness
I guess I am an American

When the Women Gather

Ever watch the women?
How they laugh?
bend from the waist
Like
wind make wheat do.

They listen chile
deep
all up in they whole selves?
They be smilin'
All them molars and wisdoms showin'
Like Cheshire cats
They be cookin' too
Season fish
fry
serve fresh squeezed lemonade

Legs wide for best air
bras relaxed on the floors
"Rules...sit out on that porch and wait!"
they say
"We busy"
Yep they be busy too
Sewin' highlights
Makin' quilts of days to come and gone gone
They be singin' too chile

'Bout all them good convulsions
those sweet sweats
those screamin' yeses
the lacks of
yep,
They be cryin' too

hand holdin'
doctorin'
sewin' raggedy edges
It's beautiful chile
Truly
"But don't rush"
They say
Don't rush
Gone head on outside

You'll know fo yo own self soon enough

Mrs. Bird

Nokia walked in high heels
Long before crawling class was through
Everybody knew she would
But folks didn't take no kind of precaution
Cept prayer
    and a few beatings
And since her mama cries in her sleep now and Nokia daddy gone
She
on
her
own

Nokia got dreams though
Dream about money and grooves
She say she wanna be a singer
Can't sing none
Thought everybody could but not her
She ain't found her mind yet so her voice is out the question
It is her booty that's the problem

I'll say it
Her ass
all sweet round firm
high too
a sculpture
crafted way back when her ancestor mother ran just for the running
it's more than she deserves in my opinion
too soon for all that in my opinion but ain't nobody ask me
must be the milk
I ain't no baby so I don't drink da shit
Somebody said I should
On account my hind pot don't rise to every occasion no more
    but

my husband stay rubbing on me
(he he)

I hear Nokia fun though
Fun to any tall male with twenty dollars
She like tall
Her daddy wun't tall
She figure that'll make a difference
It don't
She'll learn
Or maybe she won't last that long
I kinda hope something will take her out ta her misery
She sad but she don't even know she sad
I tried to talk to Nokia yesterday but she say her momma sleep and
close the door
I knock
But Nokia don't answer

She pretty
A real beauty but not that American way
That Euro way
She pretty like her ancestor mother
She hate it though
Wish she had that cream color like my niece got
But my niece ain't pretty one bit
Just light
Yellow hair weave all down her back
Color contacts in her eyes
Hmph

I think my niece toad ugly
But I don't say that out loud
On account of people's feelings

But Nokia sho love my niece
I can't stand that piss colored girl my sister make
But I wish I could get to Nokia though
Her poor booty leading her life
Way deep past the street lamps
And right to where the speak ez's turn deadly
Lord Lord Lord
Everybody tell me mind my business
But
That's the problem
We all minding our business
And barely that

Independent Woman (for Gia)

Today is her day
She will lounge in her house
In her bathrobe
In her slippers until 2 pm
Maybe 3
Watching talk shows on her TV.
Laughing at their problems
Cuz their problems are sooo different
She will paint her nails
Give herself a facial
And keep her answering machine on one ring
She will pick from the messages
With whom she will spend her independence night
Maybe Mike cuz he like to eat the sweetest sweets just right
Or Scott because he's been blessed with the butcher's cut
Or Santo becuz he likes to listen
Or maybe she'll just stay home and cuddle with her damn self
Either way it's fine because her mind is filled with her options
Her choices
Her maybes
It's fine cuz her desire is filled when her libido calls
It's fine becuz there is room for another
But only when she's in her mood for her type of love
Today is her day.
And that's just the way she likes it.

Independent Woman
(for Gia too)

John Coltrane peers from his framed home above her four-post bed
Remote in one hand
Clitoris in her right
Fingering the buttons gently as the man and woman on screen fake
    moans
        the way the director has ordered
She likes this part
Play—rewind—play
Play—rewind—play
Again her usual Friday/Saturday night
She claims to like it this way
No man hassles
No bullshit
No stress
No emotional pain she claims
But pain
(She forgot to cut the nasty hangnail on her right finger)

With her left hand
She pauses her moving and licks the right hand trying to remember
    the last time
She tasted herself on someone else's lips
Trying to remember the last time she heard herself say YES RIGHT
        THERE
OH YES THERE AGAIN
PLEASE
But she says she likes it this way cuz her fingers don't need store-
bought protection
affection
Or direction

She unconsciously gets up to put on her sexy pink teddy
Just in case
By some chance
Some old one will stop by and say I MISS YOU CAN I STAY?
But no one is cumming tonight but the people paused on the screen
cuz her body is tired of feeling its own digits
and she's turned everyone else away with her badass attitude
stemming from fear of being hurt again

The only satisfaction she'll get this night will be from the Ben &
Jerry's Chunky Monkey in the freezer
Tomorrow she plans for Coffee Häagen-Dazs
and The Lion King
But she claims she likes it this way
Her heart is lonely
Her skin is deprived
Her body is hungry
and she knows it
but she yells to me and everyone who cares that she likes it this way
and we need to be more like her.

Let It out

There is a robe she never washes
Thick and red, soft and fluffy
Terry cloth robe that hangs behind her bathroom door
Deep scented with past soaps
Yesterday's perfumes
Fried chicken and moments

She wears that robe
The loops low so the belt hangs funny around her high waist but
she wears that robe
Thick and soft when good friends come to share the reality they laid
Or did with their man or memorized for their children
She wears that robe
Soft and comfortable
Oversized and relaxing
After a lover has pleased right and left at the right time
She wears that robe to polish her thoughts
Wrap herself in the memory of his warmth then again,
All by herself, cum long and definite

She wears that robe
Easy and free
When her candles are lit and the phone is pushed ringless
When Nina, sweet Nina
is singing (young, gifted and black)
When her mother's memory is replayed
When the trees are heavy with snow
When it's time to lay down
Sit down or stand up and cry
loud and unashamed
She will listen to her heart
and let it out on canvas
on page

She lets it out in clay, in steel
She lets it out
And brings in her sanity
Then after all this, she will take her favorite fruit-scented soap and
wash her body with her hands, feeling the woman of her
She will take her ten free fingers and comb her free hair to style and
when she is done
She will place her robe
Thick and red
Soft and fluffy
Back on the hook behind her bathroom door
And laaaaaauuuuugggggghhhh.

Stacia

She LOOOVES her ganja
Visit a healin' everytime she inhale
Hold
Release
She finds a quiet place
A calm
a sorta quality
She finds a reminder of home
She deep inside her head
Where the world can't reach
She closer to God now (she thinks)
In her way and her speech
She feel a sorta peace
A justified release after the boss say
Stay late
but knows
She'll always get paid less than the old boys make
Take all you can't take
Give all you can give then
fake a smile while your teeth ache from the clench
She hears his thoughts in confidence
She a old soul

Yeah she loves HER medicine
Takes small puffs rolled in one point five paper
She sucks on Now and Laters
Strawberry her favorite kind
Ideas for real
A long and outrageous line
The big and tiny
The magnanimous and the shiny
Those that save all mankind
she thinks

She gets inspired
When she's higher
Her mind feeling all present
All tangible cider
So her cramps don't come so hard
And her back won't pain too stiff
She slides deep inside this feeling
Away from the shit
Even for a minute
She'll take it
Cuz this world is heavy baby
Thick and odd to hold
She say she need a little high to help with the cold
And it ain't gon be nose candy
Or heat in her veins
It ain't gon be no acid
The very name seems strange and lame
It's gonna be her ganja and her God
And she ain't willing to change
For you or you either

Young Ms. Russell

Afternoon
Sun shines and she stink
Cuz she don't wash and she don't care and I know that is extreme but
she don't
Got her dirt weed
Fried rice, chicken wings
Plus a cellular phone
Living in her mom's house
Spray Lysol when her mom gets home
She don't want to go
Anywhere
She wasting the life and I know this is extreme but she is

The Addiction (for One of the Bravest Women I Will Ever Know)

I am recovering she says
Recovering from an addiction
All began with a man missing
And a mommy screwing uncles
Always uncles with dollars for kisses
Always happy to come then disappear
The addiction, I will call it, caused me to beg she says
I was asking
Imploring mommy to make my daddy come
And one day

He come

Clothed as a man
Different from the uncles
Eating a fresh tomato dashed with salt
He stayed
Big man with big hands
Drank alcohol like earth holes drink rain
He stayed
Angry man
Loved to sneak behind and slap quickly
Called this man "uncle daddy"
Till mommy can't take him no more
Can't take him being mad no more
Can't take him being mean
Being broken somewhere too
And we run
We run late in the night to the very place she run from
And we stay

And we safe
But I was growing she says
Growing growing growing growing
Titties all thick
Legs all thick
Shaped like they grown but I ain't
Mostly got some things to know
But I don't before the addiction starts
Before my nipples ache
For kissin'
For touchin'
I burned them rubbing with soap she says
Then with lotion
Had to run cool water down my nightgown at nights
And while I lived there in the dizzy
Mommy up and give up
Just got swallowed
Began to rest in the eerie place
Wouldn't get up
Slept too much
Got no comfort in the child she received
Mommy just left she says
Right there but left
Leaving her baby woman to fend for herself
And make her own sins

The addiction became wild she says
Feeling
alone
unloved
made me respond when the predators
began to call
They whistled

They woofed

Must have had a scent between my legs she says

The new moist

The fresh wet and they came to get it with promises of time

With talk of my beauty

My breath

My sexiness

Young dumb and full of cum they say

My addiction breed whorishness

Stuffed and puffed with "freedom" to disguise the truth

And the truth is

Mommy needed her a plan

Mommy needed her a fan to cool down at night

Mommy needed her a kickstand to keep her upright

Mommy needed to hear the call and see the flashing red lights

And I needed me a mommy

One that could see past her own misery so I could see

So I could claim my body

So I could flourish in my own sexuality

Instead of having a

Fuckin' addiction

D u a f e

It's not like this everywhere you know
Without the television predetermined to soap operas
And videos hoes
We talk here
Or not
Depending
We get loud sometimes
Laughing and trickling our truths in the air
Smells like sweet oils
And Occasionally,
Well-seasoned black-eyed peas
The mother is there too
to remind us to hug
as we enter
Make our next appointment
as we leave
We mouth our curses cuz she there
Even as we are grown and paying
We are not as grown
We play music here
Fela and Portishead
"Do you Want More?"
And "Bizarre Ride"
We listen and think
Make faces when the crown is pulled
into Queen Dom
It feels wonderful
And so very familiar

Duafe Series #2

Brown
Nutmeg
Flesh so smooth
Mouth for talking
She don't use

Busy thinking
'Bout what?
Can't say
She speaks
Another language
Could be
Maybe

So many dialects from home to choose
Bet hers is pretty too
A roll of the tongue
Clicking sounds
Swahili croon
I don't know
But I bet it's pretty though

Today 4/4/00 (My Birthday)

Didn't wash

Didn't style, brush or grease my hair

Didn't eat right

Didn't iron my clothes

Didn't match them either

Didn't brush my teeth

Didn't make my bed

Didn't answer my phone

Didn't check my email or messages either

Didn't open a book

Didn't turn on the TV

Didn't even try to find a good radio station

Didn't do nothing

But be my funky self

My Mother Loves Me

Been a loved child all my life
So I am unafraid

My time is indefinite
I know this
So I move
Directly forward when I can
Zigzags
potholes grow
melodies capitulate (fall off)
But she loves me
Such a faith in a life
She makes me believe
So I write and she needs me to be
Life so filled with tragedy
So many solid pleasures

I write and she is woman again
Not patchwork doctor
Not neighbor
Not niece
Not daughter
Just woman
No license
But drives in her own way
She cries when she sees me
Holds me close when she knows I need me
"Mommy" I say
"Mommy" I say
Smells so good
Reminds me to go out and play
Makes me strawberry lemonade
Opens my child to me

Made my smile pretty

She so smart

"Broken and lean times

Potato soup is delicious I find

When you know what music to play

And how to set a place

And what pretty flower goes with gray"

A genius—gentle and tender

Loyal

Life giver

Naps during the day

For this

I write you poetry

Short story

Because I know you love to hear me think

And I'll sing because you love to hear me pray

And if not a body buys my books

Or sings along

My mother loves me

Been a loved child all my life

So I am unafraid

Tree Like She (for Grandmothers Everywhere)

How many times have you heard the infant cry?
How many leaves have you lost to fall?
How many secrets held?
How often, the dead weight of castrated boys on your arms?
How many younglings lost in the name of lesson?
How many generations?
Fire from fire
Storm from storm have you stood with your feet clinging
And your bones crying for lie down?
How many poets rest their backs against your frame?
Tree How many dances danced when the wind blew
Or the water tumbled,
Or the sun looked and the snow painted?
How many names carved in your heart?
How many lovers rock sweet and right under your blessed shade?
How many moons?
How many knives?
How many destinies have you seen get wet?
And yet you are constant
painstakingly healing and swelling from your greater providence
You have seen the earth green and fresh
Turn to synthetic
Yet you grow
Through the fences
Through the concrete
Through wire
Through rapid obliviousness
Through hatred swept in a neat piles

I watch you sway in the October breeze
and am
up
lifted
everytime

Carried Away

I wasn't ready to be your mother
Your main and only source of support
I wasn't prepared to give you all you needed
All that I wanted to give
But I had always dreamed of when I would be
When I could be your mommy
When I would know your smile
The red, yellow, brown of your skin
The texture of your hair
The innocence in your eyes
I dreamed of when I would know your scent
The red alarm siren in your cry
The warmth of your little presence
I always dreamed that I would show you the world
Educate you about it and the world I try to create for you
I had always dreamed of you
I always wanted you
But you came too soon
My pockets and my body just weren't ready for you
So you left
Without notice
Without preparation
Without choice
Gone
Just gone
I never had the chance to acknowledge you while you were here
With me
And there is still the nagging grief
For you whom I did not meet
Gone
Gone before I had the chance to say hello

One of the Reasons (for the hoe on the corner)

His stiffened rod of manly flesh
Roughly stabs my tonsils like excited lies waiting to explode
My head rhythmically bobs up then down as a sweet coercion for him
to spill his ten dolla load

His sexual snot leaks from the side of my lip as we both sit
Me—clearing a tattered throat
He—watching his tip...
Drip

I ask for a sip of something strong and wet to cover my pungent cum
stained breath
He offers me nothing but money that's owed and quickly guides me
to the back door of his uptown

"See you later baby," I say as the door slams in my face
I turn then walk hearing the sounds of locks locking keeping people,
like me,
Out

But damn
Just that quick,
There he is
Another sorry as trick
The light clicks
He likes my lips
Overworked and thick
But he asks for the cunt and you know customers get
What customers want
So
He pulls out his piece and I reveal my dry crease for his to savagely

enter

Back alley

cold cold in the dead of winter

But it don't matter to him

or to me

He's getting his shit off

I'm thinking about the extra I need

7:50 am

7th one's frustrations are spilling

This ain't no kinda trip

This a mean and brutal bitch

But I get paid with the switch of a fat round

Onlookers shaking their heads

Quietly with my eyes

Sometimes a finger

"Fuck you" cuz this pays the rent

My life is

Lonely

Crooked

And bent in ways those gospel girls cannot understand

I belonged to their church

Pastor the pimp

Whole congregation of hoes

Givin' all they got

I used to be just like them

Pretty dress

Fava shoes

No time for tears

No times for blues

Potato salad gotta be made

And laid on the table

"It might be deep but I keeps it light"
Reverend almighty savior says
In clean white polished and manicured
Hair cut so tight
Took me into the back room and had me all night
PAIN
PAIN IN MY SOUL
PAIN ON MY SKIN
PAIN IN MY EYES
PAIN FROM ALL THE OUTS
PAIN from all the ins
I was 14 years old
and now...
I'm fifteen

The Truth About Annana

She got a whole lotta people behind her
Father and Mothers, teacher and doctors and such
She got people
Looking
Feeling her way
And there ain't no thank you
but in prayer and action

Strides
she strides
Walks and glides cuz they watching and feeling her way
She got people watching
Not the o o old white man behind the desk
Sitting solemnly on canvas
Lining the hallway
They up deep
somewhere
come out when the rhythm is played and she dancing
Zimbabwe
Simply
Without even noticing
No pay by dance person taught her
She gone away
back
into
somewhere before
The moves regurgitate into play
and she back there somewhere

She know where

She got alotta people behind her
past her pockets of afro sheen

the American rotten pie
She got "something"
Impossible to describe
eyes don't articulate what she beams
I try to tell um
She more than collagen lips
locked hair
She more than sizable hips
dick temptation
She more than attitudes from yellow to gray
Aw ights
Player
Girlfriend
Home ay
Tareeka
Black boyfriends
Jewel ray
Shant'e
If I knew her song I wouldn't sing it to you

She got alotta people behind her

V

POETRY 4 POETS AND FOLKS
WHO WOULD LIKE TO BE

Pocket Size #2

Equality does not equal equal
If it's not divided equally

Sarcasm and the Woman Poet

If I wear a blue dress
Light blue
Soft blue with short cut sleeves
And a high hem
Will you tolerate me then?
Will you sit long enough to hear my prose?

Well, what if I let my ankles show?
Wear high heels, you know,
The strappy kind men seem to like
And paint a bright white flower on my big toe?
Will you invite me over for tea and chat?
Will I be fly enough then for that?

Well, what if I curl my hair with hot rollers,
Deep-fry it Sunday chicken style
And make my smile so wide that it scars my face
What if I wore bright red rouge
And reeked from Parisian perfume
Will I then be sexy enough to write?

Well, how about a girdle
Or a holster that plumps my breast?
What if I say real easy words with slow but comfortable stress
While I bat my lashes and fail my tests?
What if I put my hand on my hips?
Pop my neck
Roll my eyes like I did a million times before this line?
Then can I be a heard?

What if I write to win?
Win then write to win?
Do it all over again next Friday night?

Keep them clapping with punch lines

And acting

Then can it happen?

Can I then speak of struggle?

Write of disengaged values and missing respect?

Can I then hold the mirror in front of your eyes and challenge your
   seat at the head of the table I bought in front of the food I made?

Can I speak of abortion and lonely insides?

Can I talk about freedom so close to touch but too far from our
   sights?

Can I be rough and angry with my thesaurus by my side?

Can I be brash and brazen full of myself and pussy pride?

Can I scratch the chalkboard each and every time you write about
   your big dick and your tongue style?

Can I then speak and write?

Can I then think and think?

Express and confess?

Can I then be all of me or do I have to get a Ph.D. for your respect?

Because it seems you refuse to hear my voice until I'm gray and poor
   and tired of writing for craft's sake

I am quietly resigned not to do all that you like

But I have made you some cookies darling

I hope you like snake

How To

Let Truth do its thang
    Cuz the people are hungry
Burnin', twistin', cryin', dyin', for the real deal
These craving rush open doors for monsters
Toxins
      to kill
the throat
The lip
The mind
and sits like old fester
Come on man
    The people are hungry
Beggin', pleadin', screamin', fiendin' for the good stuff
For the funk trunk
For the stink and the soul in it
For the new new school
For the entrée
And they ain't gon skimp on the check.

Untitled (listen)

According to popular opinion,

I may be or not be a beautiful, insightful or intelligent person but I
    do be

Feeling

Hurting

Working

Thinking

Laughing

Loving

Learning

Crying

Cumming

Fighting   •

Smiling

Living till I be dying

Woman

Poet

Listen

Listen

Listen

One Little Hope

I wanna make reflections out of recycled paper and words
I need to write myself all over you
I want you to see my beat
And choose my hardback
Cuz I gots to wipe shredded eraser from my lap
It's what I do

I want chu to put a decorated mark in me
So you can find your way back
Nestle your soul in the pillows of me
So we can relapse
again and again
On beaches
In bathtubs
I hope you will still browse through my pages
even after you've read all the words

I Will Write

I will write
Ina way that will surprise you
Shock you and offend
Ignite and impregnate
Some
It is the cause and the purpose my sweets
Poets must think and re think

I will write
Ina way that will make you love me
Well some of you
I am thinking
Think too
You must not always agree
You must not believe me higher
I am a poet
This is my job
I will write

Words

I find myself
So often amazed by you
How bad and broken
Bent and bullied you are
You gyrate in my mouth
Trek all down my spine
Pacify and explode
You are somethin'!

You
So phunky in lonely solitude
Or laid out in a lovely string
You
Astonish me with your sounds
Your rhythms
Your absolute ambivalence
You are so agile
You are somethin'!

You
Flutter my diaphragm
Dance on my thorax
Nestle under my tongue
Remove the rough from my feet
You
Nurture my spirit
You are rhapsody
Pushin' me to exhaustion
Then replenishing
You are somethin'!

You
Bloom and pollinate

Crease with the wind
You summer, spring and rise with the children
You are Ebonics baby

You
Rub and drink me
Caress and entice me
You
Fondle and fuck
You
Knock me to my knees
Raise my right hand high
You
Build and fill me to vibration
You are somethin'!

You got me smilin'
and cryin'
Wigglin' my toes
out loud
You got me high struttin'
and deep thinkin'
You got me breathin'
and searchin'
Findin'
My
Liberation
You got me hooked baby
You are
somethin'!!!

A Poet's Home

Please tell me there is someplace
Someplace where
The words are not corrupted
Where the ego has left the building
Left the atmosphere
For the moment
Someplace
Where
The word stands
Investigating
Contemplating
The life
And the life in the word

In the word
All the joy
And the lust
The passion
And the power
The love
The humanity
Stands up through the word
For the word
Not the career chances
Or the ewwws if I say this poem
Or the possibility of being laid
Paid, praised dot dot dot etcetera
Somewhere
Someplace where
The craft is the mission and the mission is the pleasure
Please tell me there is someplace

Someplace where
I can
Just
Be
A
Fucking
Poet.

Haiku #7

Don't like fruit cocktail
One juice mixed with all that fruit
I like my own juice

To My New Lover (Written on March 27, 1993)

For the first time I've allowed someone, no you, to strip me of all my
clothing, all my confusion, all my doubt, all my fear of love
and life.
I am Naked. Yes naked. Butt naked and
Impressed with your ability to see me,
To see ME
clearly
through my private, lonely haze.
You touch me.
You feel me and make me tremble with the possibilities of
tomorrow, the next day, the next day and forever baby.
With you,
I feel my cloud cleared
my rain washing me.
With you
my flower blooms in December cold
With you
I lose mental chaos and gain tranquility.
You have my power and when I grow weary,
you replenish me.
With you
my angry ocean sits placid easy calm
With you
I have become
My entire self.

Thank you.

$8 Seat (Poetry Night)

I watch what you say
I see as the words dance from your lips toward
The sky
I fly with you
Over the careless air
Over high
Through bleak and necessary failures
Through malevolent loves
Bring me back to the crux

Please

I am your servant
Listening
With ears
Warm and tender eyes
Rub
Go on
Spill your nectar thick sweet
Knock me up
Impregnate
Fill me with dreams of things both more and mine
Go on
Recapture
Taste me
Rapture
Me
PLEASE
Hold my mind
Wring it round your thought
Let it fall loose some time
So I can breathe free
Ride me

Watch me move forward
In my seat
Then as you will
Bring me back to me
My heart roaring loudly
(Yes Lord Jehovah)
Feeling so deep
(Thank You!)
My troubles are stumbling
Running in fear
Down the streets
Away from all revolution
All cry strident
All soft feeling
All glorious reflection
All strength
My troubles are running away from the revolution in me

Unaware

They are clapping
I blink and am noticing
My hands
Revolt against me
They know more than clapping is just
So I stand
And
I
Raise my hands
And
I
Weep.

We the People

Almighty King GRIOT
Queen POETESS
We the people want to step
      back
Toward fresh
ness
We want more than taste
test
We want to digest
NOW.

LOVE our minds
With skill
With your stories
Categories unlimited
Creative + talented.

Come on B
We want more B
Than wrist
Than shine
The sum of your dimes.
The rims that rewind
When the car stops
Playin'

We the people have spoken

Music

It is the sad song
the good fight
It is the means of salvation
That instant embrace
The pungent chord
The public sexiness in the key

It is that rapture
That demanding emancipation
the baby crying
that angry pulse
the rolling of the eyes
the brick being thrown
the loud and silent middle finger

It is stating
how we feel
what we do
how we fight
the scars we wear
the violence unseen
the blacks
the purples
the pinks
the green
It is magic without the wand
Without the hat or the suspended lady

It lives

Passing from fingers

To pen

From mouth

to altar

it is

Life

Once Upon a Time

Once upon a time the poets stood
And the people could not breathe let alone bob their heads
Listening, hearing, responding to the words the poets read
Action words
Reactionary
Revolution
Hurt
Love
Life words
Joy
Death
Birth pain words
Experience a movement
Space, time, rhythm,
Living
In the consonant
The syllable
Texture, depth, tone, touch
Touch of the word
Where it falls in the hips
How it lays across the tongue
The smell of the shit
The pronunciation
How it sits
All of it

Once upon a time the poet stood
Now the poet sits
Talking like somebody else
Claiming poet because they memorized it
Some poet else's mood
Some poet else's phrase
Hit the way they hit

Revolution will be open to the public and the word is here to spark it

So rise up Wordsmith

Paper and pen

Mind to soul to body

Let go ya self

Give in

Let the words flow through you

Let it slap your booty for the jiggle

Let it do you

Move you

Come through you

Let the word prove you

Let the word prove you

Let the word prove

you are a poet

The What-ifs

It is

The

What-

Ifs

The magnanimous possibilities of this life

This now

This hour

This minute

The next is unknown

And that is ok!

Alright

All good

Uh-huh

Can't say what will break through

Can't say what will slide out

Knock up the world today

But I am soft and strong

Willed and passionate

My dreams are of seeing and being

More than what I am

And these dreams don't take the low podium

Now that I know

What I know

And that don't fit into sizes

Or parameters

Nothing can bar my exceptionality

Won't be wearing the silver medal

No medals at all

My muscle has grow and my back has vigor

I am ready for the unspecified

Why shouldn't I be?

It is the what-ifs my darlings

That we should gild

The magnanimous possibilities of this life

This now

This hour

This minute

The next to be unknown

And that's ok!

Oh yes!

All good

Uh-huh

Hallelujah